O IGUANA!
MY IGUANA!

Herbivore Is Beautiful

ANDREA SCARSI

DEDICATED

To All Animal Lovers

CONTENTS

ANDREA SCARSI

DESCRIPTION

Suppose you love iguanas, O Iguana! My Iguana! tells you everything you need to know to handle and care for your pet Iguana in the best way possible. It offers a brief overview of the Iguana as a species, a peek at the life of the wild Iguana in its native habitat, how to create the perfect habitat or iguana enclosure, and how to feed them properly. Iguanas are peaceful, herbivore reptiles and easy to look after.

They're primarily wild animals that long for tropical rainforests' wide-open, arboreal spaces. They come from there and will seek some of the comforts of their natural homes, even in captivity. That's all. When you know how to provide the needs of these majestic and, at times, gigantic lizards, they will reward you with an active and relatively long life in captivity. Iguanas can live up to twenty years if you care for them.

O Iguana! My Iguana! covers all of this and a lot more. Whether you're a beginner or want to improve your handling of these lovely reptiles, this book is for you.

NOTE OF THE AUTHOR

The Author strived to be accurate and complete when creating this book. Nevertheless, he affirms that the contents expressed in it are solely the result of his knowledge, experience, and competence in the considered discipline and does not guarantee and declare at any time that these are absolute and unequivocal.

While he made all attempts to verify the information in this publication, he assumes no responsibility for errors, omissions, different interpretations, or experimentations of the subject matter herein.

Any perceived slights of specific persons, peoples, companies, or organizations are unintentional.

There are no guarantees of performed results or income made in self-help books and manuals, as one expects. Readers must rely on their judgment about any single circumstance and act accordingly.

This book does not pretend to be an official medical, dietetic, psychological, religious, legal, commercial, accounting, or financial professional source. The Readers must seek the services of competent professionals in all the abovementioned fields.

Enjoy.

I HATCHED AN IGUANA
(From *Pearls Of Wisdom* By Andrea Scarsi)

Long ago, three years before finding myself a vegetarian, I was on vacation in Tulum, Mexico, to visit the famous Mayan watchtower over the gulf. I stayed with a family where I rented two hooks for my hammock in a room with lots of hooks. It was a fascinating and unexpected circumstance, entirely out of my usual lifestyle, and I was in the seventh heaven, despite the discomfort. The few rustic, village houses were by the sea, and one of them was a restaurant. It had a beautiful terrace with an old wooden banister looking out onto a small creek overflowing with lobster carcasses. The menu was varied and, from what I understood, comprising all the local specialties and Mexican ones in general, among which, of course, crawfish, tacos, and chicken, were standing out.

At lunch, I am fascinated by the chicken soup that I had seen one native eating. I ask for it and get it in a large bowl with copious slices of meat, skin, and bones I did not recognize like chicken, at least not as the chicken I knew. It was all different, but the taste and texture corresponded. While I eat, I talk to a tourist next to me, telling her about my impressions and concerns. She answered by saying that she had heard that where we were, people were eating the iguana, because it tastes like chicken, and that was probably the content of my soup.

To that say, it comes immediately to mind many giant iguanas I had seen on the beach in the morning, as a typical local fauna, and a shiver runs down my spine. They were so many and gigantic, strolling on the seafront as hosts. Someone also told me not to get too close to them because they could become aggressive if they felt disturbed or threatened. Meanwhile, without inquiring any further, to retain the benefit of the doubt, I had finished my first and last Mexican chicken soup, relegating the memory of that lunch in a remote corner of my mind, where it couldn't do any damage in case of a recall. I keep my holiday and deliberately forget about that fact for years, still knowing that my memory of that event was present and active, with its emotional charge somewhere in my subconscious. I didn't know whether to feel bad, guilty, or arrogant; it was the shiver's recurrence that I did not want to experience.

Years later, as a seasoned vegetarian, I know that the Iguana is a herbivore reptile that cannot survive in the absence or replacement of its specific food. I immediately feel a sense of affinity, solidarity, and partaking, and the memory of that abnormal chicken soup returns to the surface of my consciousness with the addition of a new ingredient: the awareness that the Iguana, the herbivorous reptile, is a part of me and like me. We're sharing the same nutritional fate and food attitude, the same lifestyle and way of doing and being in the sun. It's a stunning, growing revelation! Until just before I believed herbivores were only among mammals, now I know they're everywhere, built in any race and kingdom, part of cosmic destiny. That kinship I felt for the Iguana has given rise to the desire to learn more about the customs and needs of these fellow travelers when they are in nature and in our company, to learn their stories and life language to consolidate further the glory of living under the same sky and fed from the same earth, the two inseparable aspects of the one.

ANDREA SCARSI

INTRODUCTION

Before you take care of any animal at home, you need to have at least a baseline knowledge of the species. You don't need to run to a vet to discover a species; this type of information is already widely available. In this section of the book, I'm going to share some necessary scientific information regarding iguanas, so you know what you are bringing home.

Now, the first thing that you have to know about iguanas is that these critters are reptilian, which means two things: one, they reproduce by laying eggs and, two, their activity level and metabolism go down when it's cold. So, if you are not prepared to create a suitable habitat at home (temperature-regulated), iguanas might not be the perfect pet for you, as these animals have precise requirements for them to thrive as pets in your home.

The most common species sold in pet shops are the green Iguana (scientifically known as Iguana iguana). Iguanas generally prefer warmer territories and are naturally arboreal (which means they like climbing trees all day long). Unlike other reptiles, the Iguana is exclusively herbivorous, so you have to be careful when buying pellets or other commercially prepared food items for "herps" or reptiles.

You must feed your herbivorous reptiles with suitable food. Failing to do so will eventually affect your pet's health, and it may well be its ticket to an early death if you are not careful. As the Iguana's primary caretaker, your tasked responsibility is to ensure that the lizard's habitat and daily meals are ideal, or close to perfect, so your lizard won't have to say goodbye prematurely.

Although the most popular species is the green Iguana, that doesn't mean that you are limited to green specimens. Green iguanas come in a myriad of colors, from green and blue, to green and brown. Of course, some iguanas are bright green; these are the ones that we often see in pet shops. Regardless of the color (or species), all iguanas have the following characteristics:

They have a distinctive row of spines emanating from the head and continuing down to the lizard's tail, the presence of a parietal eye located at the center of the lizard's head, and large scales on the neck of the lizard (called tuberculate scales).

Iguanas can be extremely agile reptiles if they feel the need to flee from danger, and it's hard to find these critters out in the wild because the color pattern (and texture) of their scales blend perfectly with plants, grass, and tree bark. So, even if an iguana is a striking and distinct creature, it's challenging to find a wild specimen in a forest because it has a natural camouflage that protects it from potential predators.

ESSENTIAL FACTS ABOUT THE GREEN IGUANA

Green iguanas are considered the giants of its genus and can grow up to two meters (more than six feet!).

A full-grown and well cared for green Iguana can also attain the massive weight of five kilograms (or just over 11 pounds). Five kilograms is enormous when compared to the typical weight of other pet lizards.

According to recent statistics, iguanas kept as pets often have a very short lifespan — the average lifespan is only one year. That is due to poor care.

No way that's going to happen to your pet, so you need to create a suitable environment for it, and you also need to provide proper daily nourishment, because those two factors dictate whether or not your Iguana will survive in your home.

Wild iguanas are found usually in the Caribbean, some parts of Mexico, and of course, in Central America, where forests are lush and the species can truly enjoy wast, arboreal landscapes.

Wild iguanas rarely venture down from their arboreal abodes; they usually only go down to reproduce.

Unlike some lizards, iguanas are more active during the daytime.

Adult iguanas are known to survive falls from as high as forty feet.

Iguanas may look frail and a little crooked to some people,

but that doesn't mean they're completely helpless. Razor-sharp teeth and an agile and robust tail help the iguana fight off fierce predators in the forest.

Like other lizards, the tail of the Iguana can fall off if a predator grabs it. The Iguana will be able to grow another tail afterward.

In the wild, a disease-free adult iguana can live up to 20 years! Bright green iguanas are decidedly a crowd favorite.

UNDERSTANDING THE LOCAL PET TRADE

A significant number of iguanas fly in from Central and South America every year. Last century, the demand for pet iguanas boomed so much that over a million flew to foreign countries. Most of the pet lizards sold in pet stores came from Central and South America; we're talking about really faraway lands, i.e., Ecuador and Peru. You can imagine the cramped conditions that wild-caught captive iguanas had to endure on the way to the world. Today, the handling method hasn't changed much; what you see in pet stores nowadays are mainly tired, wild reptiles that yearn for the vast, arboreal landscapes of their native lands. I'm not saying that you shouldn't purchase one, but with these facts in mind, be prepared to invest in your new pet. These creatures, to become companion animals to humans, were taken away from their native habitats.

Nowadays, not all iguanas come from other countries. Still, there is a large volume of imports, but pet stores depend more on local productions compared to years ago. Soon people learned how to breed them, and iguana farms sprouted not long after the import of iguanas increased. While there is a move to buy local, if you are going to purchase locally-bred green iguanas to get a healthier specimen, you will probably be disappointed, because most large-scale iguana farms rarely take good care of their samples. So, buying a locally-bred iguana does not guarantee that your pet will live longer.

Remember, the steady destruction of forests in Central and South America places the species Iguana iguana under a threatened species classification.

Exporters must seek special approval from the authorities before capturing and shipping green iguanas to other countries. Therefore, it's legal to purchase a specimen imported legally. Don't worry about buying a green iguana – it's legitimate, only buy one if you are passionate about reptiles and ready to go the extra mile to keep them alive. A green iguana, removed from its natural habitat, still have some precise requirements. Its needs do not change, changing the environment, and if you do not cope with meeting them, it's easy to imagine what happens next.

WHAT'S IT LIKE IN THE WILDE?

To understand why your iguana has specific needs in captivity, it's best to understand what it's like for an iguana to be in its natural habitat. Below is a simple activity timeline that describes how a wild green iguana would live in its arboreal habitat:

As the first-morning sunray touches the face of the forest, the green iguana begins to wake up. In its current state, it still needs to regulate its body temperature manually, so it will move up and find a suitable branch to bask on.

The green iguana will move up to a branch that visibly has high exposure to sunlight. The iguana will stay on this spot until it feels that it has warmed itself sufficiently.

When the iguana's body temperature finally reaches an adequate level (usually after a few hours of just basking in the sun), the lizard will then empty its digestive tract of yesterday's waste.

Once the iguana has emptied its digestive tract, it will then proceed to forage for food. Foraging can take a great many hours, depending on the size of the green iguana, and the forest area that it can safely traverse.

The life of an iguana may sound carefree and straightforward, but it's full of challenges. For one, iguanas have to find enough food to last the day without being harassed by more giant adult iguanas.

Male iguanas also have to be extra careful when crossing new areas, because giant male iguanas may have already claimed that territory in which case a fight will ensue.

Before sunlight disappears, the iguana will have to finish foraging and bask in the warm light to heat its body. Higher body temperature is needed to ensure proper digestion of the food that it was able to collect throughout the day.

Before heading to its nightspot, the iguana must be able to regulate its body temperature sufficiently; otherwise, it will not benefit from all the food it has eaten.

In the wild, more massive and older iguanas usually have a better chance of successfully foraging than smaller specimens. Smaller iguanas have to fight for foraging areas; otherwise, the more giant green iguanas will drive them out.

Mating season signals the doubling of male iguana activity. Males are on the prowl for female iguanas. On the other hand, female iguanas are on the alert for aggressive males (so they can avoid or escape them).

Male iguanas have to be assertive and active during mating season; otherwise, females pay no attention to them and most likely will flee them. Females can and will outrun males if they are uninterested, even if it is the mating season!

What does this all mean for the iguana owner? The first thing you have to keep in mind is that your iguana may look "lazy" sometimes, but what it's doing is trying to warm itself enough to function and be active. Sluggishness on the part of the pet iguana may mean that it is not getting sufficient heat, which may cause a lot of problems down the road. Healthy and happy iguanas will exhibit periodic bursts of activity, followed by more extended periods of rest. That is normal. If you have several adult iguanas at home (males and females), you can expect an immediate boost during the mating season. Again, be prepared for this inevitability. Captive iguanas will try to mate and reproduce, as long as there are minimum favorable conditions in captivity.

BUILDING THE PERFECT HOME

When it comes to taking care of iguanas, no other factor is as important, or as urgent, as the habitat in which you place the Iguana. Iguanas may be more robust and bulky than other lizards, but that doesn't mean that these pets will survive harsh temperatures and lousy enclosures. Our first lesson for you (at least when it comes to iguana habitats) is that size does matter. You may love your Iguana to pieces, but if your provided habitat is too small, it won't feel loved or cared for at all. Cramped spaces are never for iguanas because these creatures are used to vast areas – perfect for foraging, hiding, and exercise. First, let's define what a habitat is. The Merriam-Webster Dictionary has two adequate definitions for this word.

The first definition is: "the place or environment where a plant or animal naturally or normally lives and grows." The second definition is: "housing for a controlled physical environment in which beings can live under surrounding inhospitable conditions." Note that we have highlighted specific phrases in the two definitions from the Merriam-Webster dictionary. We have highlighted these phrases to emphasize that habitat is more than just a fancy word for a cage. Habitat is more than just an enclosure that ensures that your Iguana will be there every day for you to admire and enjoy. A habitat is a functional space that operates independently of your broader surroundings. It must work independently because another life with different needs is living in this habitat.

So, if your surroundings become extremely cold, this habitat should stay warm. If the surroundings become extremely warm, there should be a way for the Iguana to cool itself down within this habitat. We are taking our time discussing this because many people may ask: why do our iguanas keep getting sick? Why would something that costs so little require so much stuff to survive? The reality is these creatures (unlike dogs and cats) have particular needs, and, as the owners, we have to provide for these needs so that they will survive. Human ownership does alter or manipulate, what millions of years of evolutionary development have bestowed upon these magnificent reptiles. That puts the new reptile owner in a sticky spot if he or she is not willing to work (at least a little bit) on the Iguana's requirements.

SIZE & LOCATION OF THE IGUANA HABITAT

Like most exotic pets, the Iguana is used to wide-open spaces, limitless foraging grounds, and interacting with members of its species. The life of a wild iguana is not easy, but it is free, and iguanas are always happier in their native habitats. At this point, you have to ensure that the critter will be satisfied when you bring it home so that it won't get sick and stay active.

An active iguana is a happy reptile, and you will be able to enjoy your pet iguana that much more if it is not sulking in one corner of its enclosure. Ignore the size of the cabinets in pet shops. Most of these shops don't care about the comfort of the animals they are selling anyway. A pet shop's goal is to keep the animals alive long enough for someone to buy them.

Only you can create the best habitat for your exotic pet. Do not take "advice" or "tips" from pet shop employees, because many of them are not very knowledgeable about animal care. They are aware of how to clean, handle, and feed the animals, and that's it. If you are expecting a ton of expert knowledge from these people, you will be disappointed, and it is dangerous to base all of your decisions on what a pet shop employee is telling you because you can't hold these people responsible for your pet's welfare.

Now, let's talk about habitat dimensions, and what kind of enclosure is best suited for holding an iguana. First off, don't buy or construct a large cabinet made entirely of wire or mesh. You may have seen some breeders or owners use these mesh-type enclosures, but in our experience, they are not dependable at all because mesh does not retain heat. And as you know, iguanas are reptiles, and they need heat from the environment to regulate their body temperature. They can't sweat or shiver like mammals do (sweating and shivering are essential bodily functions of mammals that allow humans, apes, and other mammals to regulate body temperature automatically), and so if you expose them to extremes of hot and cold, they won't be able to function correctly.

The ideal enclosure for iguanas is glass. Of course, glass is more expensive than mesh, but don't say we didn't warn you about the potential costs of keeping an iguana healthy and happy. But don't worry – once you have invested in "big ticket" items like the enclosure, your pet iguana will e set for many, many years.

Now, the ideal size of a glass enclosure is sixty US gallons or two hundred and twenty-five liters. That may shock many of you, but this size is necessary because it will provide the thermal gradient that iguanas sorely need to keep their body temperature and metabolism up. An enclosure this big also ensures that the Iguana can exercise and move around as much as it wants without upturning decorations and food bowls.

Some of you might be asking – what if we already have a mesh enclosure at home? The thing about mesh enclosures is that these habitats can keep the animal in, but it doesn't help keep the heat inside. That translates to higher maintenance costs because you would have to invest in 24-hour heating for the Iguana.

Remember, these critters came from tropical countries where 59 (15C°) degrees equal to freezing, 68 (20C°) degrees to breezy and crisp, and 95 (35C°) degrees to average, day-to-day temperature. It doesn't help that it's usually very humid in tropical countries, which adds to the general air temperature. If you live in a big country such as the United States, Canada, or

China, you may run into problems if you live in a state where temperatures are generally cold. Keep in mind that in the tropics, where iguanas come from, 95 degrees Fahrenheit (35C°) is just the average day-to-day temperature.

FINDING A STRESS-FREE SPOT FOR YOUR IGUANA

Let's assume that you've had a 60 gallon (225L) enclosure created specifically for your pet iguana/s. The next order of business is where to put it. Like other animals, iguanas can experience stress. As you may already know, pressure can put a constant strain on an animal's health. Stress can be a severe problem for iguanas, especially the older adults who are not as agile and adaptive as the younger iguanas. Some iguana owners choose the following locations for the enclosures: porch, backyard, and garage. The garage is one of the worst areas to place an iguana habitat. These three locations are popular with many people simply because they are out of the way. While it may sound practical to relegate your reptile to these areas, we do not recommend these areas. Here are our reasons:

First, the front and back of the house are areas most exposed to the environment. That means that the enclosure can quickly become too cold or overheated (depending on what type of climate you have).

Second, it's easy to completely forget about the iguana because these areas are out of the way. Let's face it – how many times do you visit the garage per day? The average is two times per day, and that's not enough to ensure that your iguana is doing well.

Third, areas like the garage are typically darker than other parts of your property. Iguanas need constant light and warmth, remember?

If your iguana enclosure is inside the garage, you will need to invest in proper lighting and switch off the light at night and turn it on again during the daytime. Without the artificial lighting, the iguana's natural behavior pattern and biological cycles will wreck, and that is not how you mold a healthy reptile at home. And finally, enclosed areas are toxic to iguanas mentally. They don't like to be placed in an enclosure far from the house's activity and only stare at gray walls, day in and day out.

If you have extra space inside your home, we urge you to place the glass enclosure near some windows where the iguana can view your garden or any other landscape. If you plan on keeping the iguana in a completely enclosed environment, it might be useful to install a bird feeder near the window so that local wildlife, like hummingbirds, will be naturally attracted to your iguana's show or viewing space. That takes care of what your iguana exposes to the outside. Let's talk about the activity inside your home. Do not place the enclosure where rambunctious kids or a loud, blaring television is commonplace. These stimuli are entirely foreign to iguanas, and you can be sure that these stimuli will cause stress. An ideal room is where people are just hanging out, reading, or relaxing. Don't put an iguana enclosure in places like game rooms where people go to become loud.

GENERAL HABITAT GUIDELINES

Creating the perfect habitat for your pet reptile requires so many essential details that I've decided to give them all to you in a list format for easier reading. These general habitat guidelines should always be kept in mind when you are creating an iguana habitat yourself. Iguanas are known to fight their way out of cages. Be prepared for this possibility. If you see wounds, broken nails, or even bleeding skin, your iguana has probably been trying to claw and bite its way out of the cage. This warning applies to pet owners who have acquired farm-bred iguanas, and exotic pet owners who have sourced their iguanas from places like Ecuador. The instinct to escape is constant, regardless of the source of the iguana. If you are unable to provide your iguana with a 60-gallon (227 L) glass enclosure, you need to periodically release the iguana in a protected space where it can freely scamper and climb about without being in danger of running into electrical wires or curious pets (such as big dogs). Do not purchase a massive iguana if you cannot provide it with adequate moving space! Weakness in the muscles will most certainly become a health problem further down the line.

Tiny iguanas do not require the same amount of space that massive adults iguanas need. However, we must warn you also that iguanas with plenty of food tend to grow fast and, eventually, the small aquarium-sized enclosure that was so adequate when your iguana was just a baby would no longer be suitable habitat for your pet once the iguana reaches adult size. Iguanas tend to get their full, adult size in as short as 2 ½ years. That is a relatively short period compared to other animals kept as pets. An ideal iguana enclosure would have a "basking spot" for the reptile with a constant temperature of 90 to 95 degrees Fahrenheit. The absolute minimum temperature for an iguana enclosure is 78 degrees Fahrenheit. If the temperature drops any lower than this, the iguana begins to experience changes in its metabolism. Digestion of food becomes more difficult, and movement will become limited.

An iguana enclosure shouldn't be evenly cold or warm throughout. There must be a consistently warm area and a cooler one where the iguana can retreat if its body temperature rises. Failure to provide an appropriate thermal gradient will wreak havoc on the reptile's metabolism. It's also essential to have a regular day and night cycle for your lizard, especially if you will keep it indoors. Most homeowners block off the sun with thick curtains and drapes. If your iguana does not frequently see the sun, you will be the one regulating the reptile's day and night cycle. That's extremely important because iguanas forage and feed in the morning and sleep at night. Their body and metabolism are so in tune with the sun that they cannot function normally without a proper day and night cycle.

Iguanas, like humans, require exposure to sunlight to function correctly and to stave off diseases. Sunlight is their natural source of ultraviolet light, which helps the reptile synthesize vitamin D. Reptiles such as the iguana need vitamin D to utilize it properly. UVB and UVA are crucial that the most common cause of captive iguana death is MBD or metabolic bone disease. MBD is a severe health condition wherein the iguana suffers from bone-related deformities. That poses a peculiar problem for new iguana owners. Not every home can sacrifice an ample space near the window for a big iguana enclosure, and yet, captive iguanas desperately need natural sunlight to survive. How do you manage this predicament? The solution is quite simple: create a secured enclosure outside your home (you can build it around a large tree branch if you want) and release your lizard so that it can scamper and bask in the sunlight. Of course, you would have to carefully time the release of your beloved reptile because iguanas are used to basking for several hours each day to jump-start their metabolism. UV lamps inside the enclosures are still recommended, in addition to natural basking time outside, as most owners do not have all the time in the world to devote to their reptiles. You have to make the appropriate adjustments to ensure that your lizard is still getting its daily UV requirement.

Iguanas prefer a humid environment because humidity helps them to hydrate and function better. Keep it in mind when your lizard, like an iguana, is transplanted from its tropical abode to a temperate country like the United States, Canada, or Britain. Colder countries tend to have dry air, which can cause mild dehydration in iguanas. Some reptile owners tend to think that the dehydration issue can quickly be resolved by regularly adding fresh water to the enclosure. That won't solve the problem because iguanas don't drink very much and are instinctually hardwired to depend on the natural humidity of the environment for hydration (and through the food that you provide them). A humidified enclosure will also help the iguana shed its skin. When an iguana grows, it has to shed its skin (like snakes and other reptiles) to increase size. New skin will, of course, form after the shedding.

MASTERING HEAT AND LIGHT

If you have taken care of reptiles before, you have probably heard of heating and lighting requirements. Pets such as dogs and cats are usually hardier than exotic pets such as reptiles; these animals do not require UV lamps or basking spots in enclosures. Unfortunately, the common green iguana does need these things, and you have to invest in them if you want your iguana to live a long and happy life as your companion/pet. Here is another set of guidelines, this time centering on the specifics of heat and lighting in iguana enclosures:

Iguana enclosures must be equipped with basking lights that provide adequate heat for the reptiles. Ordinary incandescent lighting setups are suitable for iguanas since the bulbs in these setups provide constant warmth at relatively lower costs. We do not recommend buying expensive heating lamps from pet stores or pet supply centers because there is nothing unusual in the bulbs installed on these devices.

If you live in a relatively cold part of the country, you may want to invest in bulbs with higher wattage so that the enclosure will be warmed adequately, especially during the night. Large enclosures should ideally have two basking spots (which, of course, translates to two lamps/lighting setups). The ideal temperature for the basking spots is 90 degrees Fahrenheit. The air temperature, on the other hand, should be no lower than 79 degrees Fahrenheit. The best way to ensure that your reptile is warm enough is by installing small thermometers inside the enclosure.

Flat wall thermometers are best. Only make sure that they are installed securely within the enclosure so your pets won't remove them. We have never recommended heating rocks to anyone who wants to take care of iguanas because these things can cause severe burns that can endanger your reptile life.

Iguanas use to heating their bodies with the help of the sun. The least that you can do as the owner is to install at least one lamp so that the iguana can function properly throughout the day. If a pet shop staff offers you a heating rock and says, "it's the norm," ignore him – he probably doesn't know that heating rocks can injure reptiles.

One of the best lighting setups for iguana enclosures is the clamp fixture. These setups are relatively inexpensive, easy to set up, and even more to adjust to create the perfect atmosphere inside a reptile enclosure.

If you have a relatively small cabinet for an equally little iguana, hard plastic fixtures are alright. But if you are planning to heat an enormous 50 or 60-gallon enclosure, you will probably need wattage in the 150 to 200 range. This kind of wattage will probably melt regular hard plastic fixtures and even cause fires in your home. The solution here is to invest in ceramic light fixtures explicitly designed to handle large electric bulbs.

Now, when you go out to the hardware store, make sure to ask for a hooded fixture, so you'll be able to attach a mesh covering under the hood to protect the bulb from any curious lizards. One never knows when a previously well-behaved lizard will suddenly feel the urge to go near an extremely hot electric lamp.

Reptiles and electric bulbs never mix well, and the risk of reptilian electrocution is high if you don't install the hooded fixture properly. As you already know from a previous paragraph, iguanas require UV light to metabolize calcium and other vital nutrients in their bodies properly. Unless your iguana has access to an open area in your backyard where it can naturally bask in the sun, we highly recommend that you purchase a separate UV lamp for your iguana enclosure.

You don't have to buy the ones sold in pet shops at all; what we are looking for in a UV lamp setup for iguana enclosures is a fluorescent bulb that provides a sufficient level of ultraviolet rays. Ask your veterinarian for a brand recommendation – he/she would know best. We don't want to recommend any brands (on principle), but what we're after is a fluorescent bulb that has been UVB-rated and recommended explicitly for creating basking spots in reptile enclosures.

Here are some tips when placing the UVB source inside the enclosure:

Find the right spot inside the enclosure where to put the light for the reptile. Ultraviolet emissions from a reptile bulb can only travel eight inches in all directions, so the bulb's height is also essential. If it's too far away from the iguana, it won't get sufficient UV rays. Lighting setups can produce lots of heat over time; UVB fluorescent installations typically do not generate heat at all, because they were not manufactured to provide light, specifically. Make sure that you can regulate the temperature inside the enclosure once the two lighting setups are installed.

Let's clarify one critical point: to help an iguana maintain its healthy metabolism and physiological functions, your terrarium or iguana enclosure will need a heat source (e.g., clamp fixture) and a UVB source (e.g., reptile fluorescent bulb).

These two things are not interchangeable; the only thing that you can substitute for these two different setups is the sun because the sun naturally provides warmth and UVB rays. So, unless you are planning to give your iguana a few hours of basking time outside its habitat, you need to invest in a general lighting setup and a UVB lamp setup. Over time, the UVB output of reptile lights tends to diminish. It's a good practice to measure all your reptile lights' output using a simple tool called a radiometer.

If you don't want to buy a radiometer and measure the bulbs' output regularly, it's best to replace the UVB bulbs every six months (up to a maximum of nine months) to ensure that your reptiles are getting sufficient UVB daily. The highest your investment in the proper equipment, the longer your iguanas live – that is awesome. If you cannot find a UVB fluorescent bulb manufactured specifically for basking iguanas, it might be a good idea to get a measurement of the UVB emission of the lamp that is available and try to install many bulbs to reach the minimum UVB requirement.

The healthy UVB emission range for an iguana is 13 to 30 W/cm2. So if you can find a UVB fluorescent brand that provided only 8 W/cm2, installing a second UVB bulb will produce a combined UVB emission of 16 W/cm2, which would then supply more than the minimum UVB requirement of iguanas. It may look complicated when you read it in this book, but it gets effortless once you get used to iguanas' peculiar needs (which isn't that different from the requirements of other pet reptiles like leopard geckos).

Do not place a plastic or glass cover over the reptile bulb, never. These materials are known to block and deflect UVB rays, so it is utterly pointless to install a reptile lamp, and then hinder it with a cover. Your iguana won't get its UVB requirement at all if you do this! You may also want to try mercury vapor lamps because these have been reported as more efficient in terms of UVB emissions. You can order some online right now if you wish.

As of the last checking, online retailers are selling MVLs online. Just make sure that you buy from a somewhat reputable online store. If you plan to buy MVLs, buy a mercury vapor lamp with internal ballast, as these bulbs are more popular with reptile breeders and enthusiasts. The reason for its popularity is quite simple: it generates heat as well as UVB. That's like shooting two birds with one stone. But be careful – MVLs with internal ballasts hare also known for higher risk of failure over time. And make sure that you read the manufacturer's instructions before installing these in your terrarium! Iguanas need a source of heat and ultraviolet emissions – these requirements are usually supplied separately as UVB setups do not emit heat.

IGUANAS & HUMIDITY

Humidity is part of the big-three requirements for raising iguanas. Iguanas have been designed by nature to live and reproduce in a tropical climate. Hot and humid forests are highly favored because these locations provide all of the things that iguanas need to thrive and flourish. The ideal humidity in terrariums (specifically, iguana enclosures) is 60 to 75 percent. This humidity level can be challenging for iguana owners who live in dry and cold parts of the country. If the air in your home is bone dry most of the time, you may have to perform some steps to ensure that your iguana is getting sufficient humidity so that it doesn't dry out (iguanas are more dependent on moisture than other animals).

There are endless ways to increase the humidity inside the iguana enclosure:

The simplest (and most cost-effective way) of humidifying an iguana enclosure is to spray the area with water numerous times per day. If you don't mind doing it regularly, you don't have to spend money on any special equipment anymore. Just spray around the entire area; the water will naturally evaporate, and the air inside the enclosure will become naturally humid. Your iguana will love it!

An alternative method (that involves the use of a spray) would be to bathe the iguana. Lightly spray the iguana twice or thrice a day. That will be its "bath," and the effect would be the same. Don't worry; the extra moisture won't cause fungal infections or molds (don't overdo it).

If your home (and your iguana's habitat) is dry, you can buy a humidifier. Just put the humidifier in the same room as the iguana enclosure, and you're all set. There are two main kinds of humidifiers: essential humidifiers (that can humidify one place) and centralized humidifiers (designed to humidify an entire house). Be sure to use soft water because tap water might contain a high amount of minerals, and this can cause respiratory problems when exposed to the white powder (the residue of humidified air) that humidifiers are known to spray. You can usually see the white powder on furniture and other stuff around the house. If you see white powder after using a humidifier for a week or so, you may have hard water running at home. Use treated/soft water instead.

If you want something dedicated to just the habitat, you may want to invest in a terrarium misting system. Install one of these, and you won't have to worry about humidity in your iguana's enclosure ever again. Of course, you will have to check the misting system from time to time, but you can do that in your routine checking of the reptile and its habitat.

Important Note:

Glass enclosures can be notoriously poor when it comes to ventilation.

Mesh enclosures are suitable for ventilation, but poor when it comes to providing a thermal gradient and sufficient humidity. If you have a glass enclosure at home, make sure that the iguana cannot escape, but at the same time, it should still let in the air. It's not a pretty sight when its habitat is slowly suffocating an iguana.

ESSENTIAL ACCESSORIES OF THE IGUANA HABITAT

Your iguana enclosure will not be a complete habitat without adequate accessories. Below is a list of the essential ones that every iguana owner should have in their terrariums:

Substrate – substrate is defined as "the base on which an organism lives." An iguana enclosure requires a substrate that will make the entire habitat more livable for the iguana. We do not recommend most of the substrates sold commercially.

Visit any online pet supply store, and we assure you there are dozens of choices when it comes to iguana substrates.

But the problem here is that 99% of the time, these commercial substrates can cause severe health problems. Any substrate formed as shavings, pellets, pebbles, etc., should be considered unsuitable for iguanas.

These substrates may be cheap and helpful in absorbing spills and waste, but in reality, these substrates can cause a variety of health issues because, whether you like it or not, your iguana will munch on the substrate.

When an iguana munches on something that it is not supposed to eat, two things can happen. First, the foreign material can get stuck in the iguana's throat, causing an impaction (which can, of course, lead to suffocation and death), or the foreign material might end up in the intestines (and the fragile digestive system can become inflamed from trying to digest the substrate).

You might be wondering right now: why would pet supply stores and manufacturers churn out bag after bag of these substrates if they were harmful to iguanas?

Well, these businesses are in it for the money, and as long as people buy stuff from them, they will continue to sell the substrates, even if the substrates are not entirely safe for iguanas.

Another issue that you should be aware of is that even if the iguana doesn't directly ingest the stuff, it can still end up inside the iguana.

When an iguana removes waste material, it extrudes bodily tissue, and when this happens, the substrate can stick to it and end up inside.

It's painful for an iguana to try to pass something that has not been broken down by its digestive system. For us, it would be like trying to pass a kidney stone.

So, how can you make sure that your iguana will be free of all these maladies associated with inappropriate substrates? Easy – use non-particulate substrates. Here are some inexpensive substrates that you can place inside your iguana enclosure:

Butcher paper

Carpeting

Synthetic grass (woven into a carpet)

Paper towels

Cloth towels

Please avoid using any paper that has ink on it, as the ink can rub off on the reptile skin.

You can use plain paper towels as a safe substrate inside iguana enclosures.

Climbing Structures – In the wild, iguanas live on trees, and rarely venture down unless they have to forage or remove waste.

These reptiles are most comfortable when they have something to climb; therefore, you must make sure that your iguana enclosure has an adequate climbing structure as the owner.

Some novice iguana owners think that small tree branches are excellent for climbing structures, but they are not. If the branches you use are too fresh, the wood will rot into mush because of the humidity control inside the enclosure.

There also might be bugs and other creatures in the wood (one never knows). Your best option is to construct various climbing structures throughout the enclosure.

We recommend wide boards and poles so the iguanas will have something sturdy to climb on. While it is true that aesthetics add to the pleasure of ownership, one must also take into consideration the weight of the reptile.

If you have a five-kilogram adult iguana, that is a lot of mass to put on a thin pole, and the reptile might injure itself as it desperately attempts to climb and exercise.

Make sure that the climbing structures that you put inside the enclosure are functional, sturdy, and aesthetically pleasing at the same time.

Take note that iguanas prefer to bask while up in the tree, so the basking spots in your enclosure should be elevated (with the help of a climbing structure) and should be near enough your sources of heat and UVB emissions.

Remember – reptile bulbs can only emit UVB up to a distance of eight inches. Remember to measure the gap between the reptile bulb (the UVB source) and the basking spot/s that you have installed.

If the basking spot is too far from the UVB (and heat source), the whole setup might not work. It's easier to adjust the UVB source/lamp and the heat source in such cases since most climbing structures emanate from a central pole (like a tree).

Hiding spot – Like humans, iguanas need their privacy, too! When the reptile feels like it's in danger, or it just does not want to be seen by humans, it needs a spot where it can be entirely out of sight (well, at least it should feel so).

You have two great and inexpensive options when it comes

to installing a hiding spot. Your first option is a large cardboard box. Cardboard boxes are great because you can take it out when it looks dirty and wilted and replace it with a new one.

The practice is environmentally friendly and easy on the pocket, too! Your second choice is a half log.

Half logs aren't exactly cheap (the large ones can cost up to $97-€90), but on the other hand, if you don't like periodically replacing cardboard boxes in your terrarium, this might be the better choice for you.

However, keep in mind that the hiding spot has to be as big as or slightly bigger than the iguana. I'm not just talking about the width of the iguana but also the length.

A full-grown iguana can grow up to several feet long, so you have to consider that fact if you want to invest in half logs, as it can get a little pricey.

Young iguanas feel the need to hide frequently (since they are small and feel more vulnerable to attacks, whether these attacks are illusionary).

The impulse to hide usually dissipates within twelve months or a year, coincidentally the beginning of an iguana's sexual maturity.

Once it reaches this peak, the need to hide slowly creeps back in until finally you are faced with an elderly iguana (as giant as it can be) that feels the need to hide just when it feels stressed or threatened enough.

Iguana cushion – You may not have heard of this particular accessory (since some people keep their iguanas in too barren terrariums), but if you want your iguana to feel comfortable, then we suggest that you put a small pillow inside the terrarium.

Just make sure that the pillow/cushion does not have loose strands, and make sure that it is adequately covered so the iguana won't feast on the actual cushion.

We also recommend that you wash the pillows regularly so they won't get filthy and unclean.

Some of you might be wondering – do iguanas have pillows in the tropical forests from where they come? Yes – iguanas have been known to use other iguanas as pillows when they sleep high atop the forest.

Adding pillows (with removable covers) in a terrarium will help iguanas settle in more comfortably during the night cycle.

Thermometers – We have already mentioned this in an earlier section – you will have to install several thermometers (at least two) throughout the terrarium/iguana enclosure to monitor changes in the enclosure's temperature.

Food and Water Containers – Sturdy dishes are a must when you are taking care of iguanas. We emphasize the word "dishes" because deep bowls are never the right choice.

The shallower the dish, the better off you will be because the iguana can reach the food and water that much more quickly.

Now, when you are filling the food dishes and water dishes, you need to fill it halfway only to ensure that the iguana won't drown in the water or accidentally dunk itself in the food.

A little food goes a long way (although it's a good idea to experiment a little as to how much your iguana can comfortably consume in a day).

DEBUNKING DANGEROUS MYTHS

Reptile enthusiasts often have good intentions, but let's face it – if there's a community surrounding a subject or interest, myths and misconceptions will mushroom. Often, these myths reach novice iguana keepers more quickly than the facts. And so we have devoted a specific section to debunking the most common myths so that you will be more informed and prepared to deal with all the stuff that you see in online forums, etc.

Myth # 1: Iguanas eat almost anything

That is a dangerous myth that has been floating around the iguana-enthusiast community for many, many years. It appears that some owners have experimented with feeding their iguanas cat food and the like. That is a horrible practice because animal protein has no place in an iguana's diet. What happens is that the iguana will eventually suffer from severe organ damage from having to process food that is not in its natural diet. We can't blame some people for this because, for many years, many authors of iguana books have claimed that iguanas can tolerate insects and such. Please, avoid this practice altogether. Unless veterinary experts state that it's safe to feed animal protein to iguanas, it's best to steer clear of it, for your pet's sake.

Myth # 2: Iguanas need to eat a bit of gravel to digest their food correctly.

That is another amazingly inaccurate myth that needs to be

debunked right now. Proponents of this myth probably base this assumption on the fact that much more giant reptiles, like crocodiles, sometimes eat stones to help crush prey such as turtles. Iguanas are not crocodiles – these critters don't even eat meat! Therefore, there is no reason for these reptiles to eat rocks so that they can digest plant matter. There is no basis in fact for this belief at all, and so it will forever remain a myth. Feeding stones or rocks to an iguana is deadly because the foreign matter will most likely cause impaction and very swift death. Forget it.

Myth # 3: An iguana will only grow as big as the habitat itself.

Some iguanas are slow to grow because of poor diet, and so it appears that it takes years before they exceed the size of their habitats. This belief is false because iguanas who receive proper nutrition can reach up to six feet easily. You'll need to reconstruct the habitat when the iguana begins to overgrow in adulthood.

Myth # 4: Hot rocks are an excellent way to heat a terrarium.

We have discussed this earlier, but I'm putting this item, here again, to emphasize that hot rocks should never be placed in a terrarium because they can burn the reptile's skin.

Myth # 5: Iguanas can be kept safely in a small terrarium.

That isn't a myth if you take care of a hatchling (or a newly hatched iguana). This statement becomes a myth if you've purchased a fully grown iguana that measures five feet long. If the habitat is not long enough, the reptile will be miserable in your care.

Myth # 6: Iguanas do not need to see the veterinarian.

Iguanas may be exotic pets, and they may have been flown in from some tropical country, but that does not mean that they don't need to see the veterinarian at all. Remember: your pet is no longer in its native habitat, and so it will eventually experience some health problems.

Myth # 7: Dwarf iguanas are best for owners who don't want giant reptiles.

Scientifically speaking, there is no such thing as a dwarf iguana. If a pet shop sold you a dwarf iguana, you were either given a hatchling or a malnourished adult. All iguanas (mostly green iguanas) can grow to several feet long. Do not be deceived by your pet's size now.

Myth # 8: Iguanas can be given to kids easily.

If the iguana recipient is a curious child with a deep passion for pets, then it's ok. But if you plan to give an iguana to a five-year-old for the "shock value," don't do it. The child may not be able to take care of the iguana at all, and adults in the kid's family may not be willing to invest in everything that needs to be purchased to make the iguana comfortable in its new surroundings.

Myth # 9: Iguanas are one of the dullest pets around.

Though iguanas may not be as active and playful as dogs, this does not mean that they are dull creatures. Iguanas are curious and intelligent animals. If they were not bright, how do you think they managed to survive forests in the tropics where prey and predators mingle in every square inch? You have to figure out how to interact with your pet and how to catch its attention.

Myth # 10: All iguanas are the same.

Each iguana has a unique personality that is waiting to be discovered. You will understand this once you purchase a second iguana. Some iguanas are passive, and some are playful, some are inquisitive, etc.

UNDERSTANDING THE IGUANA DIET

Food is probably the most crucial factor that every iguana keeper should study carefully if s/he wants to keep one's jolly reptile alive and kicking for many, many years. Now, before we roll into the main discussion, I'd like to take a step back to talk about a general misconception that people have about the iguana's diet. When we ask people, "what do you feed your iguana" they would invariably say that they feed veggies to their reptile pets. Of course, we are happy to hear that the reptiles are receiving vegetables because they are herbivorous, but eventually, this happiness dwindles as the iguana owner begins telling me that he feeds his pet lettuce 90 percent of the time.

In our fast-paced and modern society, it is no surprise that people do not know much about vegetables and their nutrient levels. But we're often surprised as to how little effort pet owners exert when it comes to choosing the plants that they give to their pets. And this lack of proper knowledge can be disastrous for the iguana because if an owner has been feeding nothing but lettuce to his pet iguana for a year, chances are the iguana will still feed on lettuce even once better vegetables are offered. Lettuce is ok (it is a vegetable, after all), but compared to other veggies available in the supermarket or elsewhere, it lacks proteins, minerals, and vitamins. It is deficient in vital nutrients. Now, we're not saying that you should avoid lettuce at all costs; what we're saying here is that you should take some time to shop for better vegetables so that your reptile will receive adequate and balanced nutrition.

Do this, and be assured that if all goes well, and your reptile does not fall ill, your iguana will live longer than other iguanas fed with nothing but lettuce. It should also be made clear that "alive and breathing" does not qualify as healthy in iguanas. An iguana might be breathing and still moving about, but that does not mean that it is robust and sturdy. You can ensure an iguana's health by providing a balanced diet, and that is what this section is all about. Now, if you want your iguana to be healthy, you have to always keep in mind that it is an herbivore. An herbivore is an animal that eats only plant-based food. Other examples of herbivores in the animal kingdom are deer, cows, yaks, buffalos, etc.

When an animal is classified as a herbivore, it means that 100% of its natural diet is plant-based, and cannot be altered to accommodate strange items such as cat food or table scraps (e.g., such as bacon). Unlike humans, iguanas are unable to digest both meats and vegetables. Although humans become healthier by "mixing it up" (eating both meat and vegetables), iguanas can become severely ill when they are fed any food with animal protein in it. It doesn't matter if the animal protein came from beef, pork, or lamb. Animal protein is the same when meat is broken down into its constituent parts. It's still animal protein, and it's deadly for your iguana. Your iguana can suffer from permanent organ failure if you feed it meat. Some people might say: well, iguanas have been observed to feed on insects in their native habitat. I'm not saying that iguanas literally cannot eat insects, but in the wild, iguanas only eat insects accidentally when feeding on plants. It is also possible that an iguana will eat an insect as a last resort if absolutely no edible plant matter is available. Does this mean that insects are a safe food item? Yes and no. Iguanas can eat insects if there is no other food available, but they can't eat them regularly. If they do, they will suffer from organ damage. Iguanas can tolerate a little bit of animal protein in the short term, to survive, but they weren't built to consume it daily.

Iguanas have sharp teeth that were designed to hook in and drag plant matter into their oral cavity. They don't chew, so don't be surprised if an iguana swallows large portions of vegetables in a single gulp. As for drinking, they do occasionally drink, but it has been observed that iguanas frequently lick water from the surroundings. So, if you are humidifying or spraying the enclosure, make sure that this is relatively clean so the iguana won't end up ingesting bacteria from its surroundings. You won't be able to dissuade the iguana from licking moisture from its habitat because, in the animal's native habitat, this is how they get their moisture. Of course, iguanas will drink from their water dish if they are thirsty, so it is still important to place a shallow water dish in their enclosure.

IGUANAS SHOULD EAT EVERY SINGLE DAY

Replace the water daily, and don't forget to wash the dish if it gets dirty. Iguanas need fresh, clean water and nothing else. Do not experiment with beverages like beer! Let's move on to the frequency of feedings. Many old books on reptile care recommend that you feed your pet once every few days, or, at the very least, once every other day. The problem with these old references is that they base their statements on very outdated information. The best practice now is to feed your iguana daily. The dietary requirements of iguanas vary from animal to animal.

Some iguanas only need to be fed once per day, while some large and more lively specimens require nourishment up to three times a day. Observe your pet, and try to determine how much food it needs daily by measuring its activity level and how much it is eating whenever you feed it. Some iguanas eat a lot in the morning after defecating and eat a little just before the night cycle. Some iguanas have been known to eat small amounts of food throughout the day. It's really up to you how many times in a day you want to feed your pet. One thing should be made clear, though – your iguana should eat every single day without fail.

THE FIRST FEEDING ALWAYS EARLY IN THE MORNING

The first feeding should always be the first thing in the morning. You can time the day and night cycle in the terrarium with your sleeping and waking schedule, although we do not recommend this if you sleep late at night and wake up very late in the day. Give the iguana most of its food in the morning and the afternoon. Limit the intake of food beginning around 5 – 6 PM because this is when the iguana's body begins to cool down as it gets ready for nighttime (sleep). We highly recommend that you feed your iguana at the same time every single day so that it will also defecate at more or less the same time the next day. Routines are fantastic when it comes to taking care of iguanas. If you have a wild-caught iguana at home, it might be difficult to coax the reptile to drink more water. Captive iguanas need a lot of water, because the surroundings are often dry, and they won't be able to seek plant matter that is naturally moist and abundant with water. If your iguana is not paying any attention to its water dish, what you can do is spray the food you give to the iguana, so that it gets extra hydration when it eats.

Just make sure that you remove uneaten food in the habitat every few hours. The vegetable matter that has been sprayed with water will develop bacteria and molds more quickly (because of the moisture). Variety is the name of the game when it's feeding time. Do not limit your iguana's diet to just cabbage or lettuce. It is usual for an adult iguana to feast on 50 different types of plant matter in the wild. That is probably why these creatures can live for 20 years if they do not become sick. If I'm not mistaken, that's like a person living up to 100 years comfortably. Another diet issue that we have to talk about is the calcium-phosphorus ratio. As you may have read elsewhere, iguanas have particular mineral requirements for bone health. Don't be alarmed – you won't have to weigh plant matter to get this ratio right. Just make sure that the calcium-phosphorous ration in your iguana's diet is 2:1. There should always be more calcium-containing food, compared to phosphorous-containing food. We know this sounds a little daunting at first, but trust me, once you have memorized which foods provide what, this will be a cinch. Vegetables like okra and collard greens are excellent for your iguanas.

Now, the following food items should only be given in moderation, because these items are known to reduce the iguana's ability to absorb calcium and iodine:

Kale, Cabbage, Bok choi, Carrot tops, Beet greens, Sorrel, Tofu, Broccoli, Brussels sprouts, Spinach, Kale, Swiss chard, Dock, Whole grain, Celery stalk, Rutabaga, Cauliflower, Beets.

THE IDEAL IGUANA DIET

Greens 40%
Other vegetables 40%
Fruits 10%
Grains, supplemental proteins, other food items 10%

ADDITIONAL DIET-RELATED GUIDELINES

Living in a big city or town, the best place to buy vegetables (and fruits) is your local supermarket. If you are not a big vegetable eater yourself, you will be surprised how many kinds of vegetables are available in the supermarket. Farmer's markets are also good, and if you want to try eating more veggies yourself, this is where you will be able to source organic vegetables and fruits. Iguanas can teach people a thing or two about healthy eating!

It is a good idea to have a stock of frozen vegetables at home, so you always have something to feed your iguana if you suddenly run out of fresh vegetables. We do not recommend feeding your reptile only with frozen vegetables daily. Fresh veggies are still the best way to go.

If you have some extra time on your hands, you may want to try growing your vegetables in your backyard. Start with one or two plants, and when those succeed, move on to more complicated vegetables (e.g., vegetables with vines). Trust me – when the fresh veggies are ready to harvest, you will love it, because you won't have to buy food for your iguana anymore and you will have fresh vegetables for yourself and your family, as well!

Iguanas can sometimes be very picky eaters. Do not fall into the trap of giving it only what it wants. Your iguana needs a variety of vegetables to thrive in a closed habitat, so even if it won't eat your mixed veggies, keep offering the dish until it bites. Do not let the iguana become the authority when it comes to feeding time!

You can try to hand-feed your iguana if you want to tame it. Do it once a week, or twice, do not do this every day. Also, do not assume that your iguana will try its best to avoid hurting you. This animal has sharp teeth, and you might end up with nasty bites if you are not careful.

HANDLING IGUANAS LIKE A PRO

One of the biggest challenges of being a new iguana owner is handling the reptiles themselves. Iguanas are not like dogs and cats, and so a slightly different approach must be taken when approaching and holding these creatures. This section will cover basic handling methods and an essential discussion on some common iguana behaviors that you will encounter as you take care of these majestic reptiles.

Small Iguanas

Many first-time iguana keepers purchase baby iguanas because they like the idea of having a reptile grow to adult size in captivity. Taking care of baby iguanas is commonplace, and it is quite possible to raise a baby to a massive adult in two to three years (if the iguana does not suffer from health problems). First, you have to take into consideration, when handling small iguanas, that these critters are incredibly active, and jumpier than adults. In terms of survival, this jumpiness helps iguanas survive hostile predators in the forest. By being jumpier than adults, small iguanas can easily confuse predators and make a run for it if they have to. So, when you are handling a baby iguana, always do it in a small, secure room with the windows and doors closed.

Doors have small spaces underneath that lizards can crawl through, so make sure you put a rolled-up towel there to cover that escape route. Trash bins should also be capped, as iguanas are known to crawl into the trash, searching for goodies to eat. Iguanas are naturally curious, and they will explore any space that they can get into. Iguanas can get stuck in small places, so be sure to handle one in a room that doesn't have many electrical sockets and hard to reach corners. Once an iguana finds a tiny spot to crawl into, you will have a hard time trying to extract the reptile, and it might get hurt during the extraction process. The worst you can do with a small iguana is to grab it haphazardly from the cage. That is not the best step if you want to tame the reptile. Always approach the terrarium slowly, and talk to the lizard gently, before picking it up.

Position your hand in such a way that you will be scooping up the lizard by its feet and torso. Do not squeeze it or hold its head. Give it a few seconds to be comfortable in your hands before playing with it. If the iguana doesn't want you to pick it up, you can stroke its spines (they're not very sharp) before attempting to pick it up again. That is a rinse-and-repeat process until the iguana becomes accustomed to you. After a few weeks, we can assure you that the iguana will remember you, and you won't have trouble picking it up at all.

Adult Iguanas

If baby iguanas are fun to pick up and play with, adult iguanas are entirely different. For one, adult iguanas are more stubborn than baby iguanas, so when you try to pick one up, it will latch on to the climbing structure as hard as possible to avoid being picked up. That is instinctual behavior, but it doesn't make this tendency any less challenging to deal with. Even though your iguana is holding on to something when you try to pick it up, we still recommend that you do it gently, so you don't injure the reptile (no matter how giant an iguana is, it can again suffer from fractures and broken claws). When approaching an adult iguana, always make sure that the reptile has seen you before picking it up. Give the iguana a few seconds to acknowledge your presence before trying to do anything. Never startle an iguana by suddenly picking it up.

Remember: these reptiles have sharp teeth and a robust and whip-like tail. You do not want to deal with a battle-ready adult iguana that feels threatened, as it will try to fight back and resist your attempts to hold it. Before even trying to lift the iguana, the first thing you have to do is loosen the reptile's grip. Loosen the front legs sufficiently before gently loosening the grip of the hind legs. When that has been taken care of, scoop up the iguana making sure that both pairs of legs are supported. Be prepared to support the entire mass of the reptile!

Iguanas are long, and when you are handling one, it's not the iguana's weight that will be tough to handle, but the shape. Iguanas have very elongated bodies and a stiff, thick tail. Over time, you will develop your unique handling style. Be observant and see what position the iguana likes best. When the adult iguana becomes very comfortable around you, it will probably use your arm or shoulder as a basking spot (assuming that you will be going out into your yard). If you are having trouble with accidental scratches, you can use a thick towel to hold your iguana. The sheet will provide an extra level of scratch protection. Do this until you have had the reptile's claws reduced or trimmed.

IGUANA TAMING TOOLBOX

Every iguana keeper wants to have a tame reptile at home, and I'm betting that you can't wait for the day when you can hold your iguana without apprehension. Well, this section is all about taming your iguana. It's called the Iguana Taming Toolbox because we will be presenting various tips and guidelines that you can use along the way. Taming is an absolute necessity if you ever plan to hold or play with your iguana. You must tame it before trying to hold it for long periods. This process is necessary to ensure that you won't get scratched or bitten when you approach the lizard. Remember, iguanas are still wild animals (even if yours came from an iguana farm), and these critters will exhibit defensive behavior if they are not comfortable with their human owners.

The first step in taming any wild animal is acknowledgment. Acknowledge that the iguana you have right now at home is a wild animal, and it wasn't made by nature to be a pet or companion to human beings. With this in mind, remember to be careful and respectful of the iguana. Don't tease it or play pranks on it just because it's sitting behind a glass or mesh enclosure. Don't abuse or mistreat it, because one day soon, the iguana will strike back at you, and you will be surprised as to how much physical pain these supposedly docile reptiles can inflict with their claws, teeth, and tail. Acknowledge, too, that these reptiles can be trained and tamed, and this will make them safer to hold. Taming is just the process of discouraging any behaviors that you don't like, such as biting, scratching, or climbing to escape through open windows.

Both old and young iguanas have to be tamed. Hatchlings are not tamed the moment they exit their shells. Baby iguanas operate more on instinct because they need to protect themselves from danger. Baby iguanas will try to defend themselves from humans if they feel threatened enough. The same thing applies to adult iguanas. If you have a giant green iguana taken from some forest in Peru, you can be sure that the iguana will be a little aggressive and territorial, and your touch will not be welcome, initially.

Your iguana must be acclimated first before you attempt to touch it. Acclimatization is defined as "the physiological adjustment of an organism to environmental change." Your iguana has to adjust first to the new habitat that you have prepared for it. Iguanas do not have this keen and inborn ability to live in small habitats. Yes, even if the habitat you have prepared is sixty gallons in size, it is still relatively small compared to the large, arboreal environment from whence the iguana has come. So, before you show off your new iguana, check to see if it's eating and comfortable in its original habitat. Signs that an iguana has acclimatized are increased activity, good appetite during feeding time, etc.

Iguanas can experience stress when you are trying to hold it and play with it. Signs of stress include:

Trying to escape the owner's hands

Sudden change in the iguana's skin color

Defecation

Loss of appetite

If you see these signs or other erratic changes in the iguana's behavior, stop what you are doing, and put the iguana back into its habitat. Make sure that the iguana has a hiding spot so that it can get out of sight. Iguanas are naturally afraid of people because, in some cases, forest-dwelling creatures in Central

America come into contact with villagers, and over time, lizards learn that villagers can mean trouble.

Some iguanas can be trained effortlessly, while some are just a pain to tame. Be patient with your iguana. If a friend has an iguana that feels comfortable with everyone, don't compare your reptile with that reptile, because the two critters may have completely different personalities.

Acclimatization is accomplished much more quickly if you remove the hiding spot for a few days. The iguana has to get used to the fact that he will be living in the habitat and, if he has no hiding spot, he will have to move around and explore his surroundings to look for a suitable place. We know – the hiding spot is there to help reduce the reptile's stress. But iguanas can sometimes hide so frequently that they acclimatize in an agonizingly slow pace – so slow in fact that owners give up trying to hold the reptile because it is taking so long. When the iguana shows signs of being completely comfortable inside its new habitat, you can bring the hiding spot back to the habitat. This approach may sound a little unorthodox, but trust me, it works. The iguana has to come to terms with the fact that it is no longer in a forest, and there is this excellent new habitat constructed just for it.

Before trying to handle an iguana, practice watching it. The iguana needs to get used to its habitat (and all the accessories that you put in there). And the presence of its keeper. To do this, sit in front of the habitat (a few feet away), and make sure that the iguana can see you. Move closer every day until the iguana becomes comfortable with the fact that you are watching it. If the iguana doesn't hide even once you are very close to the habitat, you are that much closer to ultimately taming the reptile.

When the iguana shows that it's comfortable seeing you from afar, it's time to open the habitat and show the iguana that you will not be harming or eating it. If your habitat opens from above, this might take a little longer because instinctually, iguanas feel threatened if there is something overhead, as the iguana's natural predators always strike from above the reptile. Over days, open the door and stand there, let the reptile watch you. Slowly add different elements to the equation. Touch the iguana's spines, and, eventually, you will be able to lift the iguana from its habitat.

Touching or petting an iguana is different from touching/petting your usual dog, cat, hamster, etc. Iguanas don't like to be touched too long, so during the tame phase, it's best to handle it for a few seconds or minutes and move away before it gets threatened or stressed out that you are doing what you are doing.

SUMMING UP

How Well Do You Know Your Iguana?

Reptilian pets rank sixth in the overall poll of the most popular pets in the western world at large. There are about 15 million reptile pets in the US only, right now – a staggering figure considering that reptiles were considered "strange" pets that weren't nearly as cute a few decades ago as dogs, birds, and cats.

If you want to take care of an iguana, you have to be aware that iguanas are mostly wild animals (even if you bought yours from an iguana farm), and you must treat it as such.

You must be respectful of the reptile and always be gentle and careful when handling it for the first time. Iguanas defend themselves from other aggressive iguanas and large predators; their teeth, tails, and claws can inflict injury to potential threats.

Remember that when you pick up an iguana for the first time. Iguanas have sharp claws, but they're also intelligent. Once you've been able to tame one effectively, you will hold and play with it with ease.

All you need is the right knowledge (without myths and common misconceptions), and you should be on your way to a great life with your new reptilian friend. A well-cared-for iguana can live up to twenty years!

Up Close and Personal with the Green Iguana

The green iguana (Iguana iguana) is the most popular species of iguana in the country. The boom in importing these exotic pets began to peak in the early 1990s, with over a million iguanas purchased from foreign exporters in Central America and South America.

Back then, you could be almost sure that the iguana you are purchasing comes from a tropical country such as Ecuador. People had to take care of wild iguanas that had never seen humans before, much less lived with them in a closed and controlled habitat.

Today, both private iguana breeders and large-scale iguana farms operate in the United States; this means pet shops may or may not be selling iguanas that have been imported directly from tropical rainforests.

Green iguanas are lovely as pets, because this species is the giant in its entire family of iguanas, and adults can grow to several feet in length. A fully mature iguana can weigh as much as five kilograms. Both males and females reach their sexual maturity at the one year mark.

So, if you have both male and female adults in your habitat, there is a big chance that you will have hatchlings in your midst after a few months. If your habitat is stress-free and adequately sized, hatchlings will be forthcoming, so be prepared for this inevitability.

If you only plan to take care of just one iguana, you have to make sure that the habitat you have prepared is longer than your pet and has the height needed for adequate climbing structures.

How Do Iguanas Live in the Forest?

To truly understand why iguanas require so much care, one must be aware of how these creatures live in the wild. Iguanas are hardwired to live in a tropical forest, predators, and all.

An iguana is still more comfortable living in its arboreal (yes, iguanas are tree-dwelling reptiles) environment with larger predators, than in a predator-free habitat in the city.

An iguana's day begins early in the morning when the reptile stirs from slumber. An iguana sleeps on a stout branch high above the forest floor, singly or with other iguanas.

The iguana then climbs to a suitable spot bathed with sunlight, and it begins to bask. Basking in natural sunlight is crucially vital to an iguana because reptiles are cold-blooded, and they cannot regulate their body temperature and metabolism without the sun's help.

After basking in the warm light for a few hours, the reptile will defecate (waste from last night's foraging) and proceed to forage for the day. Iguanas can eat from as many as fifty different edible plants. It may feed again before the sun comes down, but the bulk of its feeding will take place in the morning and in the afternoon.

The reptile needs to bask in the sunlight once again so it can digest its food. Without adequate sunlight, the reptile's metabolism slows down gradually. At night, the iguana finds a suitable sleeping spot once again, and the cycle repeats itself the next day.

What Makes an Enclosure a True Iguana Habitat?

There are misconceptions when it comes to taking care of iguanas. Most novice owners only have limited knowledge of what iguanas need to thrive in captivity. One of the "make or break" factors for taking care of iguanas in the enclosure, or terrarium, for the iguana.

A terrarium should not just be a cage so that the reptile will not escape the human owner. An ideal terrarium should provide most, if not all, of the reptile's physiological and mental needs.

That might sound strange to some people, as reptiles are generally thought of as mindless animals because they spend their days basking in the sun's heat.

Remember that your iguana is more intelligent than you previously thought and has particular needs to meet if you want it to live for more than a few months.

Your habitat should be able to provide heat and ultraviolet light regularly so that the iguana's physiology will function correctly.

There also has to be a structure used by the iguana for climbing and general exercise. In the wild, one must remember that iguanas are tree-dwelling reptiles that only venture down to the forest floor when they have to remove waste.

Where Should Your Terrarium Be Located?

It's easy enough to construct an ideal iguana enclosure for your new reptile(s). But the question now is where to place it on your property. Will it end up in the garage, near your vehicle or home, close to family and pets?

It's unfortunate that, over the years, people are choosing less than ideal locations for their iguana enclosures. Some owners put their terrariums in the garage; others place them outside, in the backyard.

Since iguanas are usually not everyone's cup of tea, some owners put their pets where guests will not see them as they enter the house.

I do not recommend these locations because garages can be dark, and you might tend to forget all about your reptiles when the enclosure or terrarium is out of sight.

So, the best possible location for a terrarium would be in a place such as your living room, near an open window. I emphasize the window because exotic pets like the iguana require heat and UV rays, and if you live where the sun is abundant, you won't have to purchase heating and UVB setups.

Placing your iguana near a window will also help stimulate it mentally so that it won't get bored as quickly in its new home. That will also aid in acclimatizing your iguana to its artificial habitat.

Managing Iguana Stress

You might think that your reptile isn't thinking or feeling anything significant all day long, but in reality, these majestic and massive reptiles can experience bouts of stress and depression in captivity, just like you and I would.

Iguanas are known to exhibit stress-related, erratic behavior when they feel isolated in their terrariums, or when an owner is doing something with them (e.g., holding, lifting, etc.)

Giving your pet reptile excessive stress is the last thing you want to do, because a stressed out iguana is more aggressive, and is more likely to scratch and bite than an iguana that is entirely comfortable and relaxed in its environment.

One of the primary sources of stress is the location of the iguana enclosure. If you are going to put the terrarium in a place where there is no sunlight, and there is plenty of human activity and ambient noise, chances are your iguana will experience stress continuously.

Stress can be crippling to reptiles, and your reptile can even experience early demise from losing its appetite. Another source of stress is the owner itself. For example, an owner may want to show off the new pet iguana to friends and family when they enter the house.

While this may boost a person's social status, it doesn't do anything good for the reptile, because the iguana has no time to adjust to its new environment. When an iguana is adapting, it's not just taking in the new sights and sounds – its body adapts to the new habitat.

Facing Common Situations in a Terrarium

Generally, everything will run smoothly with your iguana and its new home from day one, but some things can go wrong and, as the new iguana owner, you have to be prepared for some every day, adverse situations.

One of the most common problems that iguana owners report when they buy new iguanas is the "scratch and bite" syndrome, wherein the reptile tries to fight its way out of the new iguana habitat.

One must remember that iguanas (especially those that have been flown in from tropical countries) are used to free and wide open arboreal spaces. Wild iguanas have had the luxury of climbing different trees and foraging in various forest territories, so this behavior is not that unusual.

Common doesn't mean harmless. Be on the lookout for broken claws and damaged skin (a result of the iguana banging its head against the Plexiglas or mesh). If you are keeping several iguanas in one enclosure, you should also be prepared to deal with aggressive males fighting over available females.

If this is your first time taking care of a reptile, it's a good idea to prepare the habitat adequately before buying the reptile. Too often, people buy the iguana first, before constructing a suitable habitat.

It should be the other way around – the home should be there before the reptile comes home and also be on the lookout for erratic behavior, such as abnormal defecation patterns. That may signal disease or excessive stress.

How Warm is Your Terrarium?

Iguanas are cold-blooded creatures that require the natural light and heat of the sun to survive.

I cannot stress this enough – iguanas will die from lack of proper heat and light inside the terrarium. Unlike mammals, which can regulate their body temperature to regulate normal metabolic processes, iguanas cannot do this without basking in the sun's heat and light.

There should be a distinction between heat and light in our discussion because while ordinary light may provide warmth, that does not mean that the reptile will be getting ultraviolet rays, or UV, from the light. So if you have an iguana enclosure at home, there has to be a heating/lighting setup and a UVB setup.

The heating/lighting setup will be responsible for warming the reptile's body. It will also function to create a regular day and night cycle within the terrarium.

On the other hand, the UVB setup will emit UV rays continuously so that the reptile will be able to metabolize calcium and other vital nutrients normally, even if it is not able to bask outside in the natural sunlight.

I highly recommend that you install at least two heating lamps inside the terrarium so that the iguana will be able to choose where he wants to bask in the morning. When an iguana is basking, he is not lazy – he is warming up the machine, so to speak, to digest the food that it has eaten.

Controlling the Humidity in an Iguana Enclosure

Iguanas come from typically humid countries, where the temperature is high most of the year (77 to 95 degrees Fahrenheit) and the humidity level is a staggering 75%. In the wild, these creatures live in rainforests where humidity is even higher.

With this in mind, it's no surprise that green iguanas will require humidity control in their terrariums. You can achieve humidity control in various ways; you don't always have to purchase expensive equipment to satisfy a reptile's needs.

However, there has to be consistency in your approach to humidifying the iguana enclosure. If you want to save money, you can opt for a manual water spray. Spray the entire terrarium a few times a day to keep the inside humid.

The water from the spray will evaporate, and water vapor will mix with the surrounding air. If done correctly, this will increase the immediate humidity by as much as twenty percent.

If you can install a reliable system for humidifying your terrarium, I recommend a misting system. A misting system provides humidity control automatically. Set the machine, and it will take care of the rest for you.

You'll surely be able to find a misting setup that is timer-controlled. You can also invest in a centralized humidifying system for your whole home to be humidified (along with your iguana enclosure). These systems usually go in the basement. Just make sure that you use the recommended demineralized water for your humidifier.

Getting the Right Accessories for Your Terrarium

No terrarium/iguana enclosure is complete without the right accessories. In today's discussion, we will be discussing two essential accessories that should never be missing from any iguana enclosure: the substrate and the climbing structures.

The substrate is the material found at the bottom of the iguana enclosure. It's the "soil" that will help the iguana acclimatize to its new environment. Adding a substrate will also help the owner because it will be easier to clean the iguana enclosure if you have a substrate that acts as an absorbent mat/catcher for the iguana's waste.

If you look at the available substrates sold online to iguana owners, you will notice that many of these substrates are particulates, or are composed of masses of small particles.

I do not recommend any of these particular substrates because they all pose the same risk to iguanas. Iguanas can ingest the substrate and can end up with impactions and intestinal blockages.

You can't control everything that your iguana does within its artificial habitat, so you have to make sure that the reptile's environment will not be harmful to it at all.

Particulate substrates can also harm your iguana by getting into the cloacae cavity, which opens up when the iguana defecates. Foreign matter can get into your iguana's rear region, causing severe pain and infections. The absolute best substrate for iguanas is matted (such as synthetic grasses) or plain paper towels.

APPENDIX 1

Building An Adequate Iguana Cage

Iguanas are often touted as one of the most challenging pets to take care of due to all of the reptile requirements in captivity. Before you discard the idea of owning one, you have to understand why iguanas have these requirements in the first place. The first thing that you have to bear in mind is that iguanas are reptiles.

That means they are cold-blooded animals, and they are highly dependent on their immediate environment to function correctly. In the wild, iguanas bask for two to three hours in the sun to excrete the waste generated from yesterday's meals.

Without a consistent heat source, an iguana won't be able to eat, digest, and excrete waste. Wild iguanas are also known to spend most of their days on the branches of trees.

They rarely venture down to the ground if they don't have to because they are arboreal or tree-dwelling reptiles.

When they need food, iguanas can find as many as fifty different plants to feed on, and they get all the nutrients they will ever need because if one plant is lacking in one particular nutrient (such as calcium), the reptile will move on to the next available plant.

Tropical rainforests are incredibly abundant in plant matter; it is no small wonder that iguanas of all shapes and sizes can be found (also in abundance) in tropical territories.

If you want to build an adequate habitat for your iguana, there are a few things to keep in mind:

1. Adult iguanas grow up to six feet in length. If you take good care of your iguana, it will grow up to four feet.

Your iguana habitat has to be at least twice as long as your iguana. It is alright to start with a small aquarium initially, but over time, you will have to transfer your iguana to a larger enclosure.

Otherwise, your reptile will end up suffering in a tiny prison where it can't move around much. There is also the risk of the iguana escaping the enclosure because it has become very cramped.

2. A mesh enclosure is excellent if you live in a relatively warm area. But if you live in a state where temperatures are frigid (below 79 degrees Fahrenheit on most days), you have to invest in a large glass terrarium, because glass can keep the heat.

You will also have to install heating lamps and UVB lamps to supply the reptile with ultraviolet rays and heat. UV rays are for calcium-related metabolism. Heat is required to warm the reptile's body enough so he will be able to function well.

3. Since iguanas are tree-dwelling reptiles, the terrarium needs climbing structures in it. These have to be broad and robust enough to support your iguana. If you purchased an adult iguana around four to five feet in length, the reptile probably weighs close to five kilos.

APPENDIX 2

Caring For Your Pet Iguana

If you have just purchased your first iguana, you are probably excited and want to know how to give this great-looking reptile the best care possible. The one thing that you always have to remember when caring for reptiles like the iguana is that these fellows are incredibly dependent on their immediate environment.

If the environment is not ideal, the iguana may not grow as quickly as you'd like, and, in some cases, an inadequately regulated terrarium can also cause premature iguana deaths. Here are some basic iguana care guidelines to get you started:

1. As a new reptile owner, it's highly recommended that you start stocking up on real books that tackle proper handling, housing, feeding, and care of iguanas. They are tropical reptiles and can easily succumb to cold climates.

Learn everything about them if you want your iguana to grow to its maximum captivity size. Become a successful iguana owner and raise a giant one. You can do it when you know how to provide excellent care to these reptiles.

2. The internet is an unregulated place. Be careful when reading stuff on forums. Even well-meaning websites can provide wrong information.

If you encounter information that looks suspect, consult with a published reference, and compare the online information with printed details. In the end, your wealth of specialized knowledge will help you sift through facts and fallacies that surround the proper care of iguanas.

3. Believe it or not, iguanas feel very stressed when transported to their new homes for the first time. They use body language to communicate how they feel.

Do not hold or pat it when you bring it home. If you want to show it off to your friend, postpone that for now.

The reptile has to get used to its new home first before it can deal with the idea of being tamed. Iguanas are not used to be held by humans. There is a real risk of being bitten or hit by its tail. That applies to both young iguanas and adult iguanas.

4. Your iguana will require medical help sometimes. Before buying one, locate a veterinarian that specializes in reptiles or exotic pets in your area.

Make sure that the veterinarian's clinic is only a short drive away from your home so you can rush there during emergencies.

5. The best food for your iguana is fresh vegetables and plants. You can give it some commercial food purchased online, or from your local pet store, but please, make it a point to give your iguana a variety of nutritious vegetables to avoid suffering from malnutrition. Malnutrition is probably the number one cause of iguana health problems.

APPENDIX 3

Iguana Care

Iguanas are among the most popular reptiles in the whole world, and this exotic pet has climbed its way into the hearts of men, women, and children of all ages.

While it is true that it is straightforward to acquire an iguana (especially if you have the funds), you still have to provide a high level of care to the animal so that it will be able to live a long and happy life in its new home. Here are some guidelines to determine if you are ready to own an iguana:

1. Iguanas, like other pets, also need the loving attention of their human owners/caregivers. Contrary to common belief, reptiles do not thrive if they are plopped into a sad cage and left until the owner remembers to visit them.

2. Iguanas are mostly wild animals, and it is not in their nature to be friendly with humans. To iguanas, humans are just like potential predators in the forest. You have to take your time while trying to tame them (which sometimes lasts for as long as a month).

3. If given the proper care, an iguana can grow up to six feet long and reach the old age of twenty. Unlike dogs and cats, your adult iguana may be around until you are in your thirties, forties, or fifties!

4. Iguanas are not low-cost pets! There's a reason why these animals are tagged as exotic animals. It's not just because they come from the tropics. Proper care is needed, and the only way that you will be able to provide appropriate care is by spending a significant amount of money on the construction of its habitat, buying supplements, etc.

5. Responsible reptile owners never stop learning: they read, read, and read some more, even if they have gained a sufficient amount of knowledge to keep their reptiles healthy.

6. Iguanas need the right care from their owners, and they

also need to be in constant contact with human owners if they are to be tamed more quickly.

The problem that we see in many new iguana owners is that they are unwilling to study their new pet's specific needs. They tend to trust what the pet shop staff has to say. If you want to have a genuinely healthy pet, you have to seek the right information yourself.

You have to educate yourself and compare the various references that you come across to find the best solutions to any iguana-related problems. You also have to be willing to communicate with professionals, such as your local veterinarian, to come across issues that research cannot solve.

It's not enough to have the funds to buy stuff for your iguana. The main requirement is that you have force yourself to be a hands-on owner. Don't leave your iguana in the garage or backyard, where it can be forgotten and isolated for days on end.

APPENDIX 4

What is the Cost of Having an Iguana as a Pet?

The demand for iguanas as exotic pets has increased in recent years, undoubtedly because of more available access to pet care information, and relatively stable prices. Iguanas first exploded onto the exotic pet scene in the early nineties, and around that time, believe it or not, over 10 million iguanas had already been imported and sold around the world.

Reptiles (which include iguanas) are the fourth most popular group of pets anywhere on the planet, right after birds, cats, fish, and dogs. Decades ago, people still needed to drive to exotic pet shops and private iguana breeders to purchase these magnificent reptiles.

But today, with the boom in online commerce, people can now buy their reptiles from the comfort of their living room. Three things determine the price of an iguana: the species, size, and age.

The more exotic an iguana, the pricier it becomes. If the pet shop had to import it from Central America, the price would probably be relatively high. If you cannot afford these expensive reptiles, you may want to focus on purchasing a common iguana, or a green iguana.

Green iguanas are just as beautiful as their wild cousins imported from South or Central America. These reptiles can still grow to an impressive size – if you know how to take care of them. Young green iguanas are usually much cheaper.

If you want a large adult (around five feet in length), no questions, you will have to spend some money on it. Now, note that the cost of buying an iguana doesn't reflect how much money you will be spending on ideal reptile care.

If you want your iguana to live for more than six months or a year in captivity, you have to invest in the proper habitat and right equipment to keep your reptile alive.

Remember that iguanas are tropical reptiles, and, in the wild, these creatures are used to average temperatures between 95 and 104 Fahrenheit (35-40C). Iguanas also require a varied diet because, in the wild, a healthy iguana can eat plant matter from as many as fifty different plant species.

These reptiles have no problems with balancing their dietary requirements in the wild because they are free to roam and find the plants that they need to survive.

In captivity, iguanas are limited to what the owner can provide daily, and this alone can spell the difference between a healthy and happy reptile, and a very sick iguana with many health problems.

Unfortunately, an iguana's average lifespan in captivity is only six months because people rarely take the time to understand what iguanas need to survive.

Healthy adult iguanas can live for as long as twenty years! If you want your iguana to enjoy a long life, you need to educate yourself on what type of food it needs, and what equipment you should add to its terrarium or habitat.

APPENDIX 5

Essential Iguana Facts for First-Time Owners

Suppose this is the first time you will take care of an iguana. In that case, it is best to acquaint yourself with an iguana's biology and basic behaviors to know if something is wrong with your new pet reptile.

The first thing you must know about iguanas is that they are reptiles and, therefore, need constant heat and UV rays to stay healthy. Iguanas cannot function in a habitat with a temperature below 79 degrees Fahrenheit (26C).

UV rays are also necessary so that the iguana metabolizes calcium and other minerals. Without UV rays, your iguana will suffer from bone mineral disorders that often cause the death of these magnificent reptiles.

The iguana's anatomy

Like other reptiles, your iguana has a pair of eyes for scanning the environment for food and potential predators. It has ears protected by a relatively wide portion of skin called the subtympanic shield.

The iguana also forms spines along its back; these flexible spines are called the caudal spines and grow long and hard over time. Iguanas have a flap of skin under their lower jaw called the dewlap.

Iguanas are herbivorous (feed on plants only) with tiny yet sharp teeth to tear apart fibrous matter.

Be alert when bringing your hand near the iguana's mouth; those teeth cause severe tears on your skin. Looking closely at the iguana's head top, you will see a prominent, parietal, light patch of scale known as the third eye used to detect light changes in a given area. This primordial eye is believed to identify flying predators.

Reptilian body language

Iguanas can feel threatened quickly. Observe its body language closely to avoid being bitten or hit by its massive tail.

Iguanas will not vocalize before biting, so be careful if the iguana you have has yet to be tamed.

The dewlap, or the giant skin wad under the iguana's jowls, is to communicate. In the wild, an iguana raises its head, extending the dewlap to signal a simple hello to members of its species.

An extended dewlap means protecting its territory from the owner or other iguanas.

During mating season, an extended dewlap means I want to mate (this only applies if female iguanas are in the same enclosure, and it's the mating season).

If your iguana has been tamed and used to your presence, an extended dewlap may mean it is a little drafty and trying to make itself feel warmer.

Here are some other body language signals to memorize:

Bobbing head - I'm the big one around.

Bobbing head (to the owner) – Hello!

Bobbing head (fast) – I'm threatened and ready to fight.

Bobbing head (fast, side to side, then up and down) – I'm threatened; do not go near me!

Flicking tongue – Just exploring the air. Possibly eating something.

Flicking tongue – I'm about to take a bite out of something.

Sneezing – I'm purging my system of something.

Whipping tail – I'm about to attack.

Squirming – I do not like being held.

Head and front legs stretch – I feel good and happy!

APPENDIX 6

How to Care for an Iguana at Home

No one can contest the fact that iguanas are among the most popular pets around the world.

People love the majestic appearance of these reptiles, and they also make great pets because they can recognize their owners and know how to interact with their caregivers once they have been appropriately trained.

While the popularity of this reptile is incontestable, it is also unfortunate that only a tiny percentage of iguana owners are aware of the proper way of taking care of an iguana.

It is easy to buy an iguana because these reptiles are widely available in every country, and you can even order more exotic species to be shipped directly to your home from foreign suppliers.

However, this does not change the fact that these reptiles have precise requirements in captivity, and if the owner is not aware of these requirements, even the hardiest iguanas will only last for a while in captivity.

Let's look at the common misconceptions surrounding the care of iguanas. The common misconception is that feeding your iguana only lettuce or cabbage daily is okay.

While it is true that iguanas are herbivores and eat nothing but plant matter, they still need a variety of plant matter and vegetables to get all the nutrients their bodies need.

Cabbage and lettuce are fine, but these vegetables are very sparse in nutrients, so feeding only lettuce will probably result in nutrient and electrolyte imbalances in your iguana. So, always remember to feed your reptile a variety of vegetables daily, so it won't suffer from malnutrition.

The second most common misconception is that iguanas can use heating rocks in captivity.

While it is true that iguanas need heat to digest their food and move about in their terrariums, using a heating rock is the worst possible thing to do because your reptile can get burned from using one!

Don't listen to pet shop staff who say that it's the most popular choice because popularity doesn't make heating rocks the right choice.

If you want to provide your iguana with proper heating, install some fluorescent bulbs in the iguana habitat and ensure that you measure the ambient temperature inside the habitat. Hence, you know if your setup successfully stabilizes the temperature.

Iguanas thrive in habitats with ambient temperatures of 79 to 90 (26-32C) degrees. The third misconception first-time owners have about these reptiles is that they need low maintenance.

Iguanas can be low-maintenance pets if you give them proper daily care and if their habitat has been adequately heated and supplied with the right accessories.

You won't have to spend additional funds for veterinarian visits if you keep your pet healthy and happy. If you want the best for your new pet, saving much money for the habitat and all the other accessories the reptile needs to be comfortable inside the terrarium is wise.

ABOUT THE AUTHOR

Andrea Scarsi is a master of meditation who defines himself as a mystic, metaphysician, author, musician, and holistic coach when he uses his works to share a dimension of being, lifestyle, and knowledge founded on communion with the absolute.

Born in Venice, Italy, in 1955, he began practicing yoga and spiritism and experimenting with telepathy at fifteen. Following a near-death experience, he contacted alien and transdimensional entities at eighteen. At twenty-four, on his first trip to India, he found himself a vegetarian and in the world of meditation led by India and the Spiritual Master Osho. He received Swami Prem Sandesh as a new name, which he wears in specific environments.

He has often traveled, especially to India, residing for long periods in Nepal, the Philippines, Brazil, and Buddhist Southeast Asia: Japan, Thailand, Sri Lanka, Hong Kong, Laos, China, and Tibet. He has explored local places and cultures, met people, and participated in ritual and religious practices.

Over time, he delved into various meditative techniques for awakening consciousness, energy rebalancing, and personal evolution, which he practices and teaches. He studied philosophy and earned a Doctorate in Metaphysical Science and various diplomas, such as Holistic Life Coach, Reiki Grand Master, Master of Crystals, Shamanism, Meditation and Massage, and Wellness Coach. He's also into cellular nutrition and Network Marketing.

In 1991, he married Krisana, and they now live in Venice, Italy. Reach him at andrea.scarsi@yahoo.com and https://www.youtube.com/@ScarsiAndrea.

BOOKS BY ANDREA SCARSI

Answers For The Soul: Fragments of Eternal Wisdom
Blessings! Dedicated to Osho
Extraterrestrial Channeling: Alien Abduction Syndrome
Happy To Be Happy: The Grand Manual Of Happiness
Home Sweet Home Staging: Easy Is Right
How To Ask A Woman Out: Gentlemen Only
Indigo Crystal Rainbow and Diamond: Tell Themselves
Journey To The Underworld: First Level Shamanic
Procedures Manual
Make Your Own Vineyard: Ex Vite Vita
O Iguana! My Iguana! Herbivore is Beautiful
Pearls of Wisdom: Tales of Ordinary Metaphysics
Reiki First Degree Manual
Reiki Second Degree Manual
Reiki Third Degree Manual
Seeds Of Enlightenment: The Buddha Within
Tarot Reading Essentials: The New Basic Meaning Manual
The Art of Persuasion: How to Achieve Your Goals
Ethically
The Art of Worrying: How to Enter and Exit it at Will
The Master And The Assassin: An Ordinary Zen Story
The Secret Of Meditation: The Inner Dimension
The Secret Of Metaphysical Science: Our Eternal Journey
Through Infinite
Vegetarian Cuisine: Reasons Objections Recipes
Walking The Dogs: A Dialogue A Manual
Zen The Sense Of Nonsense: Anecdotes For Synaptic
Deprogramming

MANTRAS BY SANDESH (ANDREA SCARSI)

Mantras Maha Mantras
The Mantra Experiment
The Mantra Way
Om Namo Supernova
Amāvasya
Lingamananda

BOOKS BY ANDREA SCARSI IN ITALIAN

21 Giorni: Diario di un Ritiro Spirituale
A Proposito di Osho: Conferenze di Un Suo Discepolo
Benedizioni!: Dedicato a Osho
Benvenuti ad Atlantide: Cristalli e Chakra Riequilibrio di Primo Livello
Breve Storia Dei Sogni: Nella Visione Occidentale
Canalizzazioni Extraterrestri: Sindrome da Rapimento Alieno
Casa Dolce Casa Vendesi: Home Staging Facile
Dhyana Yoga: Unione Con L'Essenza
Dispense Reiki Primo Livello
Dispense Reiki Secondo Livello
Dispense Reiki Terzo Livello Master
Felici Di Essere Felici: Il Grande manuale Della Felicità
Felici Di Essere Felici: Seconda Parte
Guarire Il Sé Ombra: Aneddoti Di Alleggerimento Di Carico
Il Lato Positronico: Ridondanze Di Un Androide
Il Lato Positronico: Seconda Parte
Il Maestro e l'Assassino: Una Consueta Storia Zen
Il Segreto della Meditazione: La Dimensione Interiore
Il Segreto della Scienza Metafisica: Il Nostro Eterno Viaggio nell'Infinito
Il Silenzio dell'Assoluto: Satsang con Sandesh
Immagina: E Accelera la Tua Crescita Personale
Indaco Cristallo Arcobaleno e Diamante: Si Raccontano
Indaco Cristallo Arcobaleno e Diamante: Seconda Parte
La Cucina Vegetariana: Motivazioni Obiezioni Ricette
L'Arte della Persuasione: Come Raggiungere Eticamente i Propri Obiettivi
L'Arte della Preoccupazione: Come Entrarci e Uscirne a Piacere
L'Arte di Cambiare: Modella la Tua Vita
L'Arte di Invitare una Donna: Solo per Gentiluomini
Le Compatibilità Zodiacali: Trova l'Anima Gemella con

l'Astrologia

Lettura dei Tarocchi: Manuale dei Significati di Base

Massaggio Olistico: Manuale delle Procedure di Base

Menando il Can Per L'Aia: Un Dialogo Un Manuale

Notiziario Reiki: Delle Attività Mensili Svolte

Perle di Saggezza: Racconti di Ordinaria Metafisica

Risposte per l'Anima: Frammenti di Eterna Saggezza

Semi di Illuminazione: Il Buddha Interiore

Transizione Vegetariana: Per la Pecora Che si Crede Leone

Viaggio nel Mondo di Sotto: Manuale di Procedura Sciamanica di Primo Livello

Zen Il Senso del Non Senso: Aneddoti di Deprogrammazione Sinaptica

Thank You for reading
O Iguana! My Iguana!.
Andrea Scarsi

www.ingramcontent.com/pod-product-compliance
Lightning Source LLC
Chambersburg PA
CBHW071221280526
45787CB00002B/750